D0040752

I NEED
ALL THE
FRIENDS
I CAN GET
BY
CHARLES M.
SCHULZ

PUBLISHED BY
DETERMINED
PRODUCTIONS, INC.
BOX 2150 SAN FRANCISCO
CALIFORNIA 94126

PROJECT DIRECTOR:
CONNIE BOUCHER

BOOK DESIGN BY:
JIM YOUNG

OTHER BOOKS
BY
CHARLES M. SCHULZ

HAPPINESS IS A WARM PUPPY
·
SECURITY IS A THUMB AND A BLANKET

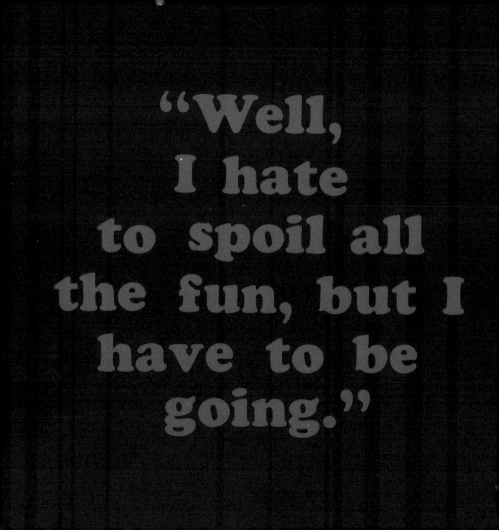

"I said, I hate to spoil all the fun,
but I have to be going."

"Sigh!"

'What's the matter with you?'

"I don't have any friends...I don't have
one single person I can call a friend."

"Define 'Friend'!"

"A friend is someone you can sock on the arm!"

"A friend is someone who will take the side with the sun in his eyes."

"A friend is someone who's willing to watch the program you want to watch!"

"A friend
is someone
who likes you
even when the
other guys are
around."

"A friend
is someone
who will share
his home with
you."

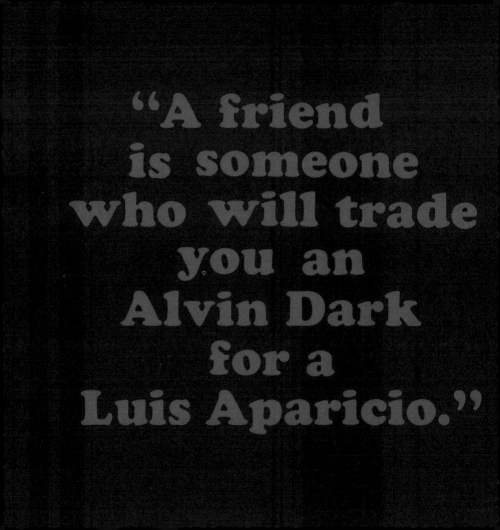

"A friend
is someone
who will trade
you an
Alvin Dark
for a
Luis Aparicio."

"I think you try too hard, Charlie Brown . . .
Be like me. I don't need any friends . . .
I'm self-sufficient!"

"Not me . . . I need
all the friends I can get!"

"I'd even settle for a 'fair-weather' friend!"

"Poor ol' Charlie Brown . . .
He really should try to be like me.
I don't care if I have any friends or not . . .

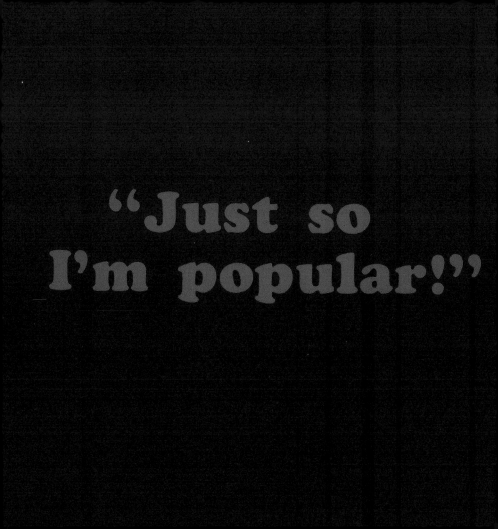

"I don't know...Talking to her
never does much for me..."

"You know what I think
a friend is, Charlie Brown?"

"A friend
is someone
who accepts
you for what
you are."

"A friend
is someone
who is not jealous
if you have
other friends."

"A friend
is someone
you have things
in common with,
Charlie Brown."

"A friend
is someone
who understands
why you like your
strawberry sodas
without any
strawberries
in them."

"A friend
is someone
who doesn't think
it's crazy to collect
old Henry Busse
records!"

"A friend
is someone
who likes the
same music
you like."

"A friend is someone who can't stand the same sort of music you can't stand!"

"A friend is someone who will hold a place in line for you."

"A friend
is someone who
sticks up for you
when you're
not there."

"A friend is someone who sends you a postcard when he's on vacation."

"A friend
is someone who
doesn't criticize
something you
just bought."

"A friend is someone who takes off the leash!"

"All these definitions
have got me confused."

" 'Friend'... A person whom one knows well, and is fond of'."

"That's me!"

"What?"

"I said, 'That's me!'
I'm your friend, Charlie Brown!"

"Well, what do you know?"

LITHO IN THE U.S.A.